# Buying and Selling

Becca Larsen

New York

Published in 2014 by The Rosen Publishing Group, Inc.
29 East 21st Street, New York, NY 10010



Book Design: Katelyn Londino

Photo Credits: Cover Yuri Arcurs/Shutterstock.com; pp. 5, 17, 19, 22 Comstock/Thinkstock.com; p. 7 Dan Kitwood/Getty Image News/Getty Images; p. 9 Wavebreak Media/Thinkstock.com; pp. 11, 15, 21 (flowers, cheeseburgers, painting) iStockphoto/Thinkstock.com; p. 11 (twenty dollar bill) PaulPaladin/Shutterstock.com; p. 13 jkirsh/Shutterstock.com; p. 21 (dresses) Hemera/Thinkstock.com; p. 21 (dolls) intoit/Shutterstock.com; p. 21 (gardening) Stockbyte/Thinkstock.com; p. 21 (babysitting) Photodisc/Thinkstock.com; p. 21 (building) Brand X Pictures/Thinkstock.com.

ISBN: 978-1-4777-2260-2
6-pack ISBN: 978-1-4777-2261-9

Manufactured in the United States of America

CPSIA Compliance Information: Batch #CS13RC: For further information contact Rosen Publishing, New York, New York at 1-800-237-9932.

# Contents

# Goods

Malia's mom is an important part of the community. She owns a small business. She sells goods that people want and need. Goods are things that are made or grown. Flowers are goods. Malia's mom buys flowers and then sells them to people in the community.

Malia learns about buying and selling by helping her mom.

# At the Market

Every week, Malia goes with her mom to the flower market. Here, **producers** sell flowers to the shop owners. Then, the shop owners sell the flowers to the community. There are many flowers to pick from. They come in many colors and sizes.

Many producers sell their flowers at the market near Malia's house.

Wholesale
Flowers

Malia's mom **invests** in buying flowers. That means she spends money to buy flowers from the producers. However, she'll sell the flowers for more than she spent. That way, she makes a profit. A profit is the amount of money someone makes after they subtract what they spent on supplies.

It's a good investment if there's a profit.

Malia sees a batch of roses. They cost $200. Her mom buys them for that price, but she'll sell them in her shop for $300. This way, she'll make a profit of $100. That's a good investment.

Malia's mom is a good business owner.
She almost always makes a profit!

THE UNITED STATES OF AMERICA
FEDERAL RESERVE NOTE
IB 32651288 A
B2
20
TWENTY DOLLARS

$300 – $200 = $100

Malia's mom sees lilies. She's not sure if she can **afford** them. The producer tells her they cost $100. Malia's mom thinks this is an affordable price. If she sells them for more than $100, she'll make a profit.

If Malia's mom sells the lilies for $150, she'll make a profit of $50.

# At the Store

Malia's mom brings her new flowers to the shop. She puts prices on them. She'll sell a batch of daisies for $20. She'll sell a batch of sunflowers for $10. People will buy these flowers because they're not overpriced.

It's important to keep prices as low as possible.
Then, people will buy more flowers.

$10

People who buy flowers at the shop are an important part of the business. They're called **consumers**. A consumer is anyone who buys something from a business. When consumers buy things, Malia's mom makes money. The consumers are thankful for Malia's mom. She sells the goods they need.

Malia treats consumers like friends. She smiles and helps them pick their flowers.

# Services

Malia's mom sells both goods and services. A service is work done for another person. Malia's mom works to make gardens beautiful for some of her consumers. In return, people give her money. The flowers are the goods and the gardening is the service.

Malia helps in the gardens, too. She likes helping people!

Sometimes people want flowers **delivered** to their house. This is another service that Malia's mom sells. She pays Mr. Jones to deliver the flowers. It's an investment because she has to pay him. However, it's a good investment because her consumers will pay more for delivery.

Can you think of more examples of goods and services?

# Examples of Goods and Services

Malia loves to help at the flower shop. She learns important things about goods and services every day!

# Glossary

**afford** (uh-FORD) To have enough money to buy something.

**consumer** (kuhn-SOO-muhr) Someone who buys goods or services from someone else.

**deliver** (dih-LIH-vuhr) To take something to a person.

**invest** (ihn-VEHST) To spend money on something in order to make money.

**producer** (pruh-DOO-suhr) Someone who grows or makes things to sell them to other people.

# Index